J. D. WILLIAMS

History of the Name
Mac CARTHY

Brian Boru Monarch of all Ireland

(Surnames became official in obedience to his edict)

HISTORY HOUSE
Ennis, Ireland.
Tel.: 065/24066

History House,
P.O. Box No. 19,
Ennis, Co. Clare,
Ireland. Tel.: 065/24066.

ISBN 0 85342 538 8

OTHER BOOKS BY J.D. WILLIAMS

History of the Name Murphy
History of the Name O'Brien
History of the Name O'Kelly
History of the Name O'Neill
History of the Name O'Sullivan

CONTENTS

Section I

Section II

FOREWORD

The bearing of the Celtic heritage upon modern civilisation, and its influence in moulding the character of the people who inhabit Ireland, the British Isles, Europe, United States of America, Canada, South America, New Zealand and Australia is not only little understood, it is scarcely dreamed of. Ever conscious of this influence, I have produced this series of the histories of Irish surnames in an effort to bridge this Celtic heritage information gap. The Irish and those of Irish extraction, be they first, second, third or fourth generation, should therefore know and proudly cherish the history of their surname, so that they may derive wisdom and resolve from a deeper understanding of themselves.

I acknowledge with thanks the facilities made available by the following: Bord Fáilte Éireann, National Gallery of Ireland, National Library of Ireland, National Dairy Council, H.M.S.O London, Minister for Foreign Affairs, Dublin, Irish Times Ltd, Irish Press Ltd, Cork Examiner Ltd, Irish Independent Ltd, Cement Ltd.

James D. Williams

SECTION I

IRISH CELTIC HERITAGE

'From the deepest sources of antiquity the history of the Irish is taken; so that, in comparison to them, that of other nations is but a novelty and a beginning'—Camden's *Britannia.*

Few, if any, will dispute Camden's dictum for the thousands of years of human activity and culture are as dramatically attested by the ancient monuments which dot the Irish countryside as by the relics housed in her museums and libraries.

The presence in Ireland today of a large number of castles in various stages of preservation or ruination justify the claims of most descendants of the Irish that they are of Royal descent; direct descendants of the Celts.

The following passage from Thomas d'Arcy McGee's poem 'The Celts' aptly describes these characteristics:

> Long, long ago, beyond the misty space
> > Of twice a thousand years,
> In Erin old there dwelt a mighty race,
> > Taller than Roman spears. . .

The annals relate that the Celts landed in Ireland around 504 B.C. and brought with them many characteristics of a civilised and courageous people, the most notable of their customs being their Clann system. This Clann (Clan in English) or family system of local government, existed from the time of the coming of the Celts, to the period of the Anglo-Norman conquest of Ireland, seventeen hundred years later. The clan system afforded every Celt the fullest personal freedom, and although the chief's power was strong, it was limited by strict laws and customs. The Celts never had the spirit of base servility towards their chiefs as characterised the mass of the people who evolved from the feudal system.

The Celts were bound by the ties of the family and they acted through the impulse of affection; the serfs or inhabitants of Feudal Europe were moved only through the impulse of fear. As a result, the ancient Irish or Celts, had no class hatred, which unfortunately was most prevalent amongst feudalised people. The love the Celts had for music and games is legendary for we are told that every third year of their calendar, the High King, (or Árd Rí) presided over 'Feis Tara', an All-Ireland National Assembly for Law, Music, Games and Literary contests. Today over two thousand years later, gaelic games and Irish music play a very substantial part in the life style of the Irish at home and abroad. It is a fact that the clan system was instrumental in moulding the characteristics of the ancient Irish and their descendants, the present-day Irish. These descendants of the Celts or ancient Irish still hold on to the many traditions and fine qualities which are uniquely Celtic. These qualities will always have a special place with the Irish, for the bright new future of tomorrow is built on the valued things of yesterday, tried and trusted things that have stood the test of time. The warmth of their welcome is historic, as are their songs. The first thing the Irish learn about life is how to enjoy it; it is a lesson nobody has to teach them, for the pursuit of happiness is deep-rooted in Ireland. Instinctively the Celtic Irish find pleasure in the simplest of things, the things they know best and longest, natural things. These, coupled with courage, physical strength and a civilised temperament, are the characteristics of Celtic heritage, which have been handed down unbroken from generation to generation.

HISTORY OF SURNAMES IN IRELAND

The history of the personal names of the people of any country is a subject surrounded with very great interest. By means of a family nomenclature, much light can be thrown on the early employments and customs of a people, as well as the sources from which they sprung. In fact, the history of our country lies enshrined in its surnames; and so a little knowledge of the early history of Ireland is useful in understanding the origins of surnames. Historians generally agree that the period of time from the Great Flood to the birth of Christ was four thousand and four years (4003 B.C. — A.D. 1). The first recorded inhabitants of Ireland were the Parthalonians from Greece, who landed in Ireland 1484 B.C. They were followed by the Nemedians, 1154 B.C., the Fomorians 978 B.C., Firbolgs 738 B.C., Dedannan 686 B.C. and finally the Celts or Milesians 504 B.C. The conflict between the Celts and Dedannan for the supremacy over the country of their adoption, gave birth to the living legends of leprechauns, for when the Celts attacked the Dedannan the latter retreated into their earthen fort mounds, which they built as their homes; this gave rise to the impression that they disappeared underground and this is the origin of the little people or leprechauns, as they are now affectionately known. The remains of their fairy forts, or earth mounds, are found in abundance all over Ireland today; there are thirty thousand officially recorded.

The mighty Celts, tall, blonde, blue-eyed, courageous and hospitable were sweeping through Europe around 500 B.C. and landed in Ireland at that time. Heremon, son of Milesius, King of Spain, 504 B.C. was one of three sons of Milesius who led the Celtic Conquest of Ireland. Heremon was also the first absolute monarch of the Emerald Isle. Milesius' other sons were Ir and Heber. Ir did not survive the Celtic Landing and so Ir's son, Heber Donn took his father's command. All the Irish and their descendants will trace their origins back to these three Celts, who ruled over Ireland around 500 B.C. The Celts established their supremacy over the whole island by the enactment of laws and regulations, which prevented any of the original inhabitants from becoming provincial kings or chiefs. The laws stated that none but the descendants of Heber, Heremon and Ir should inherit provincial thrones or that of Árd Rí or Chief Monarch of the country. For this purpose, and to ensure the Celtic continuity of power, it was necessary that a perfect record of every family should be kept, its genealogical history, the lands it possessed and its chieftains and clans. To achieve this mammoth task, Milesian monarch, Ollamh Fodhla was the first to reduce this principle to a system by the establishment of his celebrated Council held on the historic Hill of Tara. The system the Celts used for governing the country was termed the Clann system (Clan in English) or family system, it being patriarchal in its origins. The country under the clan system was divided into many small tribal kingdoms, most of which were grouped into seven provincial kingdoms. These kingdoms had a common language, common laws, and a common social structure. The High King or Árd Rí had supremacy over the provincial kings, and it was decreed by council or assembly at Tara that each chief or king should possess a Brehon or judge to: (1) See that the laws of the Kingdom were observed; (2) Record all actions of his Chief, record births, deaths and marriages; (3) Present all this information every third year at Tara for inspection and approval.

The succession to the thrones of tribal kings or chiefs, provincial kings and High King resulted from these records, copies of which were kept at Tara. The laws of the Celts showed how civilised and organised they were. The regulations regarding dress were interesting. The rank of the individual was displayed on his cloak by the number of colours he was permitted.

One colour . . . . Workmen and farmers
Two colours . . . Soldiers
Three colours . . . Officers
Four colours . . . Innkeepers
Five colours . . . . Sons and daughters of kings
Six colours . . . . Brehons and historians
Seven colours . . . Kings.

The system of naming of the Celts was termed Clan names or tribal names and these were formed from those of illustrious ancestors by prefixing a word or Cineal (English kindred, race, descendants); clann (English family, children, race); dal (tribe, progeny); ua, ui (plural); (grandson, descendant); Cineal Eoin, race or descendants of Eoin; Ui Neill, the descendants of Niall; Ui Fiachra, the descendants of Fiachra; Clann Rory, the family of Rory. The tribe consisted of many families all of whom claimed descent from a common ancestor. O'Hart in his books on Irish pedigrees, traces the genealogical history of most Irish families from these Celtic tribes.

Individual members of each family of the tribes had only one personal name, or, as we would say, a Christian name. A man's name would be simply John, or Cormac, or Niall or Donagh. If there were two or more Johns in the neighbourhood, then his father's name was also given. John, son of Patrick, and if necessary, his grandfather's name was added, John, son of Patrick, son of James. However, as their numbers grew, the existing system was impracticable for obvious reasons and it became necessary to identify themselves better. This gave rise to the formation of Irish surnames, for a surname is a family name, common to all members of the family and their descendants.

The Irish were the first people in the world to form surnames.

The manner of forming the surnames was very simple. Each member of a family had one personal name of his own such as John, Cormac, Niall, Donagh, and so on. In addition to this, all the members of a family took as a common surname the name of their father, with Mac (the Irish for son of) prefixed or of their grandfather or some distinguished ancestor with "O", (the Irish for grandson or descendant of) prefixed. Thus the O'Neills, are so called from their ancestor Niall, King of Ireland A.D. 916, and John O'Neill means John, the descendant of Niall (O meaning descendant) or Patrick O'Brien, means Patrick, the descendant of Brian, O'Briens so called from their ancestor Brian Boru, King of Ireland (1002-1014) or Peter McCormack means Peter, the son of Cormac (mac meaning son of) or Ciaran Mac Donagh—Ciaran, son of Donagh and so on. The development of such surnames was slow and spread over several centuries, but their use became general in Ireland at the beginning of the eleventh century in obedience to an ordinance of Brian Boru.

As a result of the Anglo-Norman invasion and settlement of Ireland in the twelth century, surnames acquired two forms, one Irish and one English (Anglo-Norman). In the fourteenth century, the power of English was weakened after the murder of William de Burgo, Great Earl of Ulster, and many Anglo-Norman families in Munster and Connaught spoke the Irish language and assumed surnames like those of the Irish, by prefixing Mac to Christian names of their ancestors, such as Mac William, Mac Gibbons, Mac David, Mac Raymond, and became so hibernicised that in 1366, an act was passed ordering that by statute, 'Every Englishman do use the English language, and be named by an English name,' leaving off entirely the manner of naming used by the Irish.

This statute clearly recognises a difference existing between the Anglo-Norman English and Irish methods of naming up to and including the fourteenth century. During 1465, an attempt was made to stamp out the use of Irish surnames among the Irish themselves. In 1465 a law was passed by the English Parliament enacting 'that every Irishman that dwells betwixt or amongst Englishmen in the County of Dublin, Myeth, Vriell, and Kildare. . . shall take to him and English surname of one town such as Sutton, Chester, Trym, Skryne, Corke, Kinsale, or colour, as white, black, browne; or arte or science as smith, or carpenter; or office as cooke, butler; and he and his issue shall use this name under payne of forfeyting of his goods yearly till the premises be done.'

This Act resulted in further anglicisation of Irish names, because of the different methods used by the Irish to comply with the law. The O and Mac prefixes were dropped, the dropping or adding of a letter to the original name was used, and also by translation of the surname into its English equivalent, e.g. O Mulryan became Ryan, MacHugh became Hughes, the O'Reilly became Rawleys, MacGowan became Smith, and O'Meara became Merrys. Such events as the defeat of James II by the Williamites in 1690, the Plantation of Ulster, and the Penal Laws hastened the change of Irish into English surnames, and the anglicisation of Irish names gained momentum.

Gaelic names like O Maille became O'Malley, Malia, Malie, Mallia, Mallow, Malley, Mealie, Mealy, Melia, Millea, O'Mealue, O'Mealy, and Mac Oireachtaigh became Mac-Geraghty, Geraghty, Gerahy, Garity, Garrity, Gearty, Gerathy, Geraty, Geraughty, Gerety, Gerity, Gerraghty, Gertey, Gerty, Gheraty, Jerety. These names were more easily pronounced as the English language became more popular with the influx of English settlers. It is impossible now, in some cases, to trace whether families are of Celtic or English descent, as some of the English settlers took Irish names and Irish families were compelled to adopt English surnames. *Ó* is the Irish for 'from' or 'of' and becomes *O'* in English denoting genitive case.

Because of the complex nature of the creation of surnames in Ireland from the coming of the Celts up to the present day, I have attempted a brief summary of its main sub-divisions to aid a better understanding of the history of **surnames in Ireland.**

DERIVATION OF IRISH SURNAMES

The history of the Derivation of Surnames forms an interesting branch of study, but it would be impossible within the limits of this book to enter fully into the subject, and all that can be attempted is to give a brief summary of its main sub-divisions as applicable to this country.

Surnames in Ireland may be divided with reference to their derivation into six classes, viz.:

1. From Personal Names.
2. From Rank or Occupation.
3. From the Animal, Vegetable, and Mineral Kingdoms.
4. From Locality.
5. From Personal Peculiarities or Attributes.
6. Other surnames.

1. The following examples may be given of surnames derived from Personal Names:

CELTIC NAMES

McShane   (MacShawn – Irish. Son of John)
McFadden   (MacPaidin – Irish. Son of Little Patrick)
McAndrew   (MacAindris – Irish. Son of Andrew)
McHugh   (MacAodha – Irish. Son of Hugh)
McDermott   (MacDiarmada – Irish. Son of Diarmaid)
O'Farrell   (O Feargail – Irish. The descendant of Feargal)
O'Toole   (O Tuathail – Irish. The descendant of Tuathal)
McDonnell   (MacDomhnaill – Irish. Son of Donall)
McKeown   (MacEoghain – Irish. Son of Eoghan or Owen)
McRory   (MacRuadhri – Irish. Son of Ruadhri or Rory)

Many surnames derived from Celtic Names are compounded with the word 'Giolla' – a servant (or disciple) of–such as–

Kilbride   (GiollaBridghid–the Servant of St Bridget)
Gilpatrick   (GiollaPadraic–the Servant of St Patrick)

Gilchrist   (GiollaChríosd—the Servant of Christ)
Gildea   (Giolla Dé—the Servant of God)
Gilfoyle   (GiollaPhóil—the Servant of St Paul).

Maol is also prefixed to the names of Saints, signifying a bald or tonsured person who became the spiritual servant of such Saint, as:

Maol-Dubhan (Maoldun) — the Servant of St Dubhan.
Anglicised—Muldoon.

ENGLISH NAMES

Abraham	Henry	Lawrence	Rodgers
Adams	Jackson	Mathews	Stevenson
Adamson	Jacob	Paul	Thomas
Davidson	James	Peters	Thompson
Fergus	Jameson	Roberts	Williams
Ferguson	Johnson	Robinson	Williamson

2. Surnames from Rank or Occupation. The following may be selected by way of illustration:

CELTIC NAMES

McGowan   (Gabha—Irish. A smith, son of the Smith)
McCraith   (Craith—Irish. To weave—son of the Weaver)
Breheny   (Breathamh—Irish. A Judge)
Davin   (Dámh—Irish. A Poet)
Cleary   (Cléireach—Irish. A Clerk)
McIntyre   (Mac-an-tSaoir—Irish. The son of the Workman)
Ward   (Bárd—Irish. A Bard)
Colgan   (Colg—Irish. A Sword, a Swordsman).

ENGLISH NAMES

Abbott	Clarke	Fuller	Page
Archer	Cooke	Gardiner	Porter
Baker	Cooper	Gardner	Potter
Barber	Deacon	Glover	Prior
Bishop	Draper	Harper	Sexton
Butcher	Farmer	Hunter	Sheppard

Butler	Forrester	Mason	Smith
Carpenter	Forster	Mercer	Taylor
Chandler	Fowler	Naylor	Usher

3. Many surnames are taken from natural objects in the Animal, Vegetable and Mineral Kingdoms, such as:

CELTIC NAMES

Carrick (from carraig—a rock)   Darragh (from dair—an oak)
Clough (from cloc—a stone)   Mullally (from eala—a swan)
Colum (from colum—a dove)   Quilty (from coillte—woods)
Cunneen (from coinín—a rabbit)   Sheedy (from síoda—silk)

ENGLISH NAMES

Ashe	Deer	Lamb	Sturgeon
Bird	Dove	Moss	Swan
Buck	Forrest	Peacock	Veale
Bull	Fox	Pidgeon	Waters
Chestnutt	Hare	Rabbit	Woods
Clay	Heron	Silver	Woulfe
Crowe	Hogg	Spratt	

4. *Surnames derived from Locality.* Surnames derived from locality, which in England and Scotland form a large class, are but rarely met with in this country, and in most of these cases considerable doubt exists as to whether the surname has been acquired from the locality.

The following surnames amongst others are the names of localities in Ireland:

Adair (Adare)	Cavan	Kilcullen	Monaghan
Ardagh	Cashell (Cashel)	Kilkenny	Monahan
Athy	Galway	Limerick	Pallas
Borris	Kells	Longford	

The following names of localities from England and Scotland are also found amongst surnames in this country:

Bermingham	Carlile	Glasgow	Paisley
Birmingham	Galloway	Hastings*	Peebles
Cambridge	Girvan	Lincoln	Sherwood
Carlisle			

5. Surnames derived from Personal Peculiarities or Attributes, such as:

CELTIC NAMES

Roe (Ruadh—red)	Casey (Cathaiseach—valiant)
Duff (Dubh—black)	Dempsey (Díomusach—arrogant)
Lauder (Láidir—strong)	Brody (Bródach—proud)
Daly (Dall—blind)	Corcoran (Corcurach—purple or
McGirr (Gor—short)	red)

ENGLISH NAMES

Black	Jolly	Merry	Swift
Brown	Little	Short	White
Browne	Lyttle	Shortt	Wise
Fair	Long	Small	Wyse
Gray	Meek	Strong	

6. *Other Surnames* There are many surnames not falling in any of the above classes, such as those from:

Parts of the Body: (Celtic Names): Kinnavy (cnámh—a bone); McCosh (cos—a foot). McClave (lámh—the hand); (English Names): Beard, Foote, Head, Legge.

Names of the Seasons: as Spring, Summers, Winter.

Points of the Compass: as North, South, East, West.

Natural Objects: as Field, Flood, Hill, Snow.

Other Sources: as Church, Ferry, Hood, Hunt, Kirk.

The present population of Ireland is a mixture of a number of different races in which the Celtic is the predominant element. The great bulk of the most common names in the country are undoubtedly of Celtic origin.

IRISH SURNAMES ABROAD

From the earliest historic times, the Irish have gone abroad as missionaries, as soldiers in foreign armies or as emigrants.

From the sixth to the ninth centuries, Irish monks journeyed over most of Europe, helping to restore Christianity and learning to a continent plunged into the Dark Ages by the collapse of the Roman Empire and the invasions of the Goths, Vandals, and Huns. St Columcille, St Columbanus, St Gall and others went abroad from monasteries such as Kells, Durrow, Bangor, and Derry and founded centres of learning throughout Europe including Iona, Lindesfarne, Bobbio, and Luxeuil. They brought Christianity as far north as Iceland and as far east as Kiev. It is believed that St Brendan, called the Navigator, reached the American continent.

From the sixteenth to the eighteenth century, thousands of Irishmen joined continental armies and many distinguished themselves in the service of France, Spain, Austria and Russia. After the defeat of the Jacobite cause in Ireland in 1691, eleven thousand sailed to France and formed the famous Irish Brigade which fought for France in the wars of the eighteenth century. Thousands more, driven into exile by the severity of the Penal Laws against their religion, fought in almost all the continental wars of the time.

Maurice Hennessy in his book *The Wild Geese* said that as many as 460,000 Irishmen died fighting for France in the seventeenth and eighteenth centuries. If this be the case then more Irishmen have given their lives for France than for Ireland.

We do know that Irishmen with Irish surnames gave their lives in great numbers at Fontenoy, Cremona, Marsaglia, Toulon, Barcelona, but that many of the Irish who went to Europe at that time survived and their descendants still live in Europe today.

Lord Clare was a Field-Marshal of France, George Brown of Limerick an Austrian Field-Marshal, Count Thomas Arthur Lally was the hero of Fontenoy, an O'Dwyer distinguished himself at the siege of Belgrade, Count de Lacy was awarded the highest military honours in Russia. The O'Rourkes of Breffny also distinguished themselves on the continent of Europe, for, after Cromwell, many of its ablest members left the country to become well known military leaders. In Russia, they established themselves as one of the most important families. Joseph O'Rourke, Prince O'Rourke in the Russian aristocracy was General-in-Chief of the Russian Empire in 1700. Patrick, Count O'Rourke, was a member of the Russian imperial staff in the nineteenth century. There were two Owen O'Rourkes, both Counts, who served with Maria Theresa, Empress of Austria, between 1750 and 1780. Owen Roe O'Neill was known as Europe's greatest general. These were some of the Wild Geese, who distinguished themselves. However, there were thousands more who fought and died, and whose histories will never be written, men from the rank and file of the regiments of the Wild Geese.

The Regiment of Colonel William Stanley, 1586-1604
The Regiment of Colonel Henry O'Neill, 1605-1610
The Regiment of Colonel John O'Neill, 1610-1628
The Regiment of Colonel Hugh O'Donnell, 1632-1638
The Regiment of Colonel Owen (Roe) O'Donnell, 1633-1642
The Regiment of Colonel John Barry, 1636
The Regiment of Colonel Patrick Fitzgerald, 1639-1641
The Regiment of Colonel Patrick O'Donnell, 1643-1647
The Regiment of Colonel Dermot O'Sullivan Mór, 1646-1647
The Regiment of Colonel John Morphy, I, 1646-1659
The Regiment of Colonel Dudley Costelloe, 1653
The Regiment of Colonel Charles (Cary) Dillon, 1653
The Regiment of Colonel Richard Grace, 1658
The Regiment of Philip O'Reilly, 1655-1660

The Regiment of Colonel George Cusack, 1656-1662
The Regiment of Colonel Louis Farrell, 1658-1660
The Regiment of Colonel James Dempsey, 1660-1662
The Regiment of Colonel Theodore O'Meara, 1660-1664
The Regiment of Colonel John Morphy, II, 1667-1669
The Regiment of Colonel Denis O'Byrne, 1673-1686.

The surnames of great Irish generals, Dillon, Clark, O'Neill and the rest are engraved in the façades of the Arc de Triomphe, standing magnificently and proclaiming the glory of France, and one of the avenues that lead up to the great memorial is named Avenue MacMahon, honouring Patrick MacMahon, who was, of course, President of France.

Irish soldiers gave France something more than service in the battlefield. At least two of them impressed their names on commodities, which, though pecularly French in origin, have been known all over the world for many years. That tasty sauce, Mayonnaise, derives from the Irishman, Mac-Mahon who invented it, while Hennessy, the well known brandy was first produced by Richard Hennessy in 1766. Richard Hennessy, born in Kilavullen, near Mallow, in 1720, became a captain in the French army and shared in the success of Fontenoy twenty-five years later. A more personal and celebrated success awaited him in 1765, when he established the House of Hennessy at Cognac.

The mother of one of the greatest Frenchmen of all time, Charles de Gaulle, was of Irish stock, from the MacCartans of Co. Monaghan and when he resigned as President of France, he came to Ireland to relax and pay his respects to his mother's people.

Spanish people of Irish descent are very much aware of their origin. Indeed, in 1972, an association of Spaniards of Irish origin was established, with branches in Barcelona and Madrid. The Association is named 'Wild Geese Spanish Clan', or in Spanish, *El Clan Español de los Patos Salvazes*. According to the Clan, there are three hundred Spanish surnames of Irish origin and one thousand five hundred families bearing these names today. The most common Irish names in Spain, today, are O'Donnell, O'Callaghan and O'Connor. The two most prominent Spaniards of Irish descent in recent times were Father O'Callaghan, who made important discoveries in the caves of Qumran and a General Leopoldo O'Donnell, all of whose family followed a military career.

Irish emigration to North America began after the Cromwellian Wars and continued during the early eighteenth century. By 1775, there was a substantial Irish element in the American population and several of the signatories of the Declaration of Independence were of Irish birth or descent.

Many of these earlier emigrants were Dissenters, chiefly Presbyterians from the North of the country, who suffered equally with Catholics under the Penal Laws. It was from these emigrants of all denominations that great numbers of soldiers of the American War of Independence were drawn. The really large scale Irish exodus to the United States began in the years of the Great Famine from 1845 to 1848, when the whole social and economic life of the country collapsed. The stream of emigration which began during the early eighteenth century continues up to the present day but on a much reduced scale. Apart from those who emigrated to the United States, many went to Australia, Canada and the countries of Latin America, particularly Argentina, Chile and Uruguay.

The story of the Irish in the United States is one so vast that it could fill a complete library. Many of them and their descendants rose to eminent positions and prospered in the land of their adoption.

In George Washington's Revolutionary (or Continental) Army that won American independence, thirty-five per cent were Irish. On the lists of that Army there are more than twelve thousand Irish names, five hundred and sixty of them officers.

Charles Lucy in his book *Harp and Sword, 1776* lists the numbers of some with familiar Irish surnames.

These were:

695 Kellys	231 Mullens
484 Murphys	201 Walshes or Welshes
331 McCarthys	183 Carrolls
327 Connors or O'Connors	178 O'Neills
322 Ryans	184 Fitzgeralds
285 Reillys	142 Farrells
248 Doughertys	138 Flynns
243 Connollys	108 Gallaghers
266 Sullivans	168 McGuires
231 O'Briens	165 Magees
128 Lynchs	115 Hogans.

So many distinguished themselves for bravery and military ability that it would be impossible to mention them all. Twelve of Washington's senior officers were Irishmen. Washington's secretary and aide-de-camp was General Stephen Moylan, a Corkman, and brother of the Catholic Bishop of Cork. He afterwards became quartermaster-general of the Continental Army; Brigadier-General Richard Montgomery, born at Raphoe, Co. Donegal, who commanded the expedition sent by Congress in 1775 to invade Canada, and who fell at the siege of Quebec; Major General John Sullivan, the son of Kerry parents, who in capturing Fort William in 1774, was responsible for the first victory over the British in the War of Independence. Commodore John Barry, the Father of the American Navy, was born in Tacumshane, Co. Wexford. It was he who captained the first regularly commissioned American cruiser to capture a British warship in the Revolution. A Derryman, Charles Thomson was Secretary of the Continental Congress and contributed to the original draft of the Declaration of Independence.

Eight of the signatories of the Declaration of Independence were of Irish background, three were Irish born. The three Irish-born signatories were Matthew Thornton, the Limerick-born doctor, James Smith, Dublin-born, and George Taylor, an ironmonger by trade signing for Pennsylvania. Signatories of Irish origin were Edward Ruthledge,

Thomas Lynch, Thomas McKeon, George Read, and Charles Carroll of Carrollton, who was the only Catholic signer.

When the French sent a force to help the rebel Americans, under Rochambeau, the majority of the 2,200 men were of the Irish Brigade. Count Arthur Dillon was second in command of that force, with the Irish surnames of Walsh, Roche, O'Brien and Murphy among its officers. They engaged the British at Savannah, and in the fierce battle that resulted, they suffered many casualities. Historians record of the battle that the Irish Brigade particularly distinguished itself but suffered most.

The Irish in America have been prominent in practically all spheres of men's endeavour, in the Arts, Commerce, Science, Medicine, Industry of all types, Politics and Religion. In the world of the arts Ireland gave many poets and professors to the New World, like Richard Dalton Williams, and sculptors like Jerome O'Connor, many of whose works can be seen in America today.

The Father of American Chemistry was Dr William James MacNevin, born in Ballynahowna, near Aughrim, Co. Galway in 1763. He went to America in 1805 and became co-editor of the *New York Medical Journal*. He held several professorships, and, as well as being an author of many authoritative works on chemistry and science, wrote *Exposition of the Atomic Theory*.

Michael O'Neill, born in Co. Donegal, was the first man to discover uranium in America in 1912, in Dolores County, Colorado. John Philip Holland, of Co. Clare, gave America its first submarine, in 1898. It was the most revolutionary invention of its day.

The name over the first great chain store system in America was that of James Butler, who went to America penniless at the age of twenty. Butler worked in farms and hotels, and saved two thousand dollars. He entered the grocery business in 1883. At one time, his company operated 1,350 grocery stores. The name William Grace is today a familiar one in Ireland. William R. Grace's first job in

America (after he ran away to sea at the age of 14) was on the docks as a longshoreman, and he rose to become the builder of W. R. Grace and Company, and the founder of the Grace Steamship Line.

Cork-born William Garland of Los Angeles is honoured in U.S. railway history as the sole builder of the Gala, Globe and Northern Railway (now the Globe Branch of the Rio Grande Division of Southern Pacific Co.).

John B. McDonald was one of the foremost railroad builders of the late nineteenth century. He constructed stretches of the Illinois Central and the Baltimore Belt-Line railroad, but is best remembered as the builder of the first New York subway beneath Broadway. At his death in 1911, all power was shut off on the subways for two minutes as a tribute to his memory.

John Daniel Cummins was the man who paved Broadway. He also built over four hundred large buildings and miles of streets, viaducts and gas lines. He built much of New York's former elevated railroads.

The only multi-millionaire in Toledo's history has been Denis Coughlin, whose career began when he went west as a member of a construction gang on the Erie and Kalamazoo Railroad.

It was Martin Maloney who brought light to Philadelphia. The famine of 1848 forced Maloney's parents to move to Pennsylvania. He worked his way up from clerking in a grocery to a plumbing and gas lighting business. Later, he invented a gasoline burner for street lamps. He was one of the organisers of United Gas and Improvement Co. of Philadelphia.

Michael Cuddahy revolutionised the entire meat packing industry. He went to work at the age of fourteen in the business. He later developed the process for summer curing of meat under refrigeration and became head of Cuddahy Packing Co.

Marcus Daly rose from being a pick and shovel miner to one of the wealthiest miners of the West. While working for

Salt Lake City Banking House, he saw the future in the Montana mine fields. When his advice to take over a small mine, the Anaconda, was rejected, Daly bought it himself with capital he had raised in California. Also associated with him in this venture were Ryans, Kellys and Hennessys. After the great copper strike with the Anaconda as a base, he created the Amalgamated Copper Co. a seventy-four million dollar giant.

James A. Farrell, who began working at the age of sixteen years in a steel wire mill, served for over twenty years as President of the United States Steel Corporation.

Irish surnames are preserved in the persons of many of the Presidents of the United States of America. Andrew Jackson (1829-37) was son of two emigrants from Carrickfergus. The ancestors of James Knox Polk (1845-49) came from Donegal. The father of James Buchanan (1857-61) was born in Donegal. The father of Alan Arthur (1881-85) was a clergyman from Ballymena, while William McKinley (1897-1901) sprang from Dervock, Co. Antrim stock. John F. Kennedy was the first Catholic President of the United States and had his roots in Dunganstown, Co. Wexford where his Irish relations still live. Richard M. Nixon can trace his origins to Timahoe, Co. Laois. Gerald Ford can trace his origins to Co. Longford, and Jimmy Carter's Ulster origins are already established in Derryall, Portadown.

The surnames of Irish descendants are widespread throughout Australia, as well. Some of the most eminent were: Robert O'Hara Burke, an Irishman who was one of the group to cross that great continent for the first time in 1860-61.

Rev. Daniel Mannix was Archbishop of Melbourne and was well known throughout the world for his uncompromising pro-Irish opinions. Patrick Hannon of Ennis, Co. Clare, staked his claim in June, 1893 to one of the richest gold mines at Kilgoorlie in Australia. Patrick Hannon, described as a small rugged Clare prospector is now honoured all over Australia; the principal street in Kilgoorlie, where Hannon made his discovery which resulted in a major gold rush, is named after the Clareman, and a monument to his memory stands in the town square.

Cardinal Patrick Moran, born 1830 in Australia of Irish parents was Archbishop of Sydney in 1884 and was elevated to Cardinal in 1886.

The outlaw Ned Kelly was one of Australia's most colourful characters, for he was leader of the famous Kelly Gang.

In the foregoing pages, I have shown how widespread Irish surnames are scattered throughout the world. Nearer home it is a fact that there is a bigger population of Irish surnames in England, Scotland and Wales than there is in Ireland itself.

Many thousands left Ireland to become factory workers in the great industrial cities of Britain. Large numbers remained in Liverpool, just across the Irish sea, where they had disembarked. Liverpool has a substantial Irish element in its population today, as have London, Manchester, Birmingham and Glasgow.

The Irish emigrants to England settled mostly in areas of heavy industry, where there was a need for their skills. However, the Murphys, the Kellys, the O'Briens, the Sullivans, the Walshes, the Byrnes, the O'Connors, the O'Neills, the Doyles, the McCarthys, the Kennedys, the Lynches, the O'Reillys, the Bradys, the Duffys, the Donovans, the Barrys, the Foleys, the Caseys and the rest are to be found all over England, Scotland and Wales today. The present figure of 850,000 first born Irish in England can be multiplied by four to give you an estimate of the number of Irish descendants there are in England today.

I will deal with particular Irish surnames in the British Isles in another section of this book.

ORIGIN OF THE SURNAME MacCARTHY

The surname MacCarthy or in Irish MacCarthaig derived from the name Carthach, who was an eleventh century Prince of Desmond (south Munster) who died in 1045. The MacCarthys were a powerful clan of the Eoghanacht tribe of the race of Heber, founded by Eoghan Mor, son of Olioll Ollum the first King of Munster in the third century. After Olioll's death his sons inherited his lands, Thomond (north Munster) went to Cormac Cais, (whence the Dalcassions) and Desmond (south Munster) to Eoghan. The families which descended from Eoghan were known before the introduction of surnames as the Eoghanacht, and the surname MacCarthy is derived from Carthach, Lord of the Eoghanacht who the Annals relate died in a house deliberately set on fire by one of the Lonergans in 1045. The root of the word Carthach is in Irish *Cathair*, meaning a city and Carthach implies the founder of a city. The ancestors of the MacCarthys founded the city of Cashel, which was formerly the royal seat of the Kingdom of Desmond. This Prince Carthach, son of Saorbhreathach (anglicised Justin) was a grandson of Ceallachan Caiseal who was King of Munster about the middle of the tenth century. His son Muireadach called himself Muireadach MacCarthaigh, a name which has become one of the most numerous in Ireland, and was the father of the celebrated Cormac MacCarthy, King of Munster in the twelfth century. It is interesting to note that the Irish names of Saorbreathach together with Fingin and Cormac were used for centuries by various branches of the MacCarthys; however, their anglicised forms of Justin, Florence, and Charles are now more common. The MacCarthy family motto is *Forti et fideli nihil difficile* meaning 'To the

Brave and Faithful nothing is impossible.' Another motto is sometimes used — *Fortes ferox et celer* — meaning 'Bravery is fierce and swift.'

There are three main divisions of the MacCarthy family in Munster:

1. **The** MacCarthy Mor branch in Kerry with its seat at Muckross near Killarney.

2. **The MacCarthy** Reagh branch located in Carbery, **West Cork.'**

3. The MacCarthys of Muskerry located in Mid-West Cork with its seat at Blarney Castle.

The Castles of the MacCarthys are in evidence all over the Province of Munster and remains of the principal ones can be seen at Muckross, Aglish, Lissanure, Strugrena, Blarney, Carrignavar, Timoleague, Macroom and Kanturk.

MacCarthy is the most numerous of all Irish surnames with the prefix Mac, meaning son of. Out of every hundred MacCarthys in Ireland, sixty of them live in County Cork. There are 25,000 bearers of the name resident in Ireland at the present time. However, we must not forget there is possibly ten times that total of MacCarthys living outside the shores of Ireland; in the two Americas, Canada, Australia, New Zealand, England, Europe and Africa, and the rest of the world. There is a MacCarthy family in every county in Ireland, but the main branches of the family are associated with counties of Cork, Kerry, and Tipperary.

THE MacCARTHYS OF MUNSTER

The Eoghanacht possessed Desmond, or south Munster, the present-day counties of Cork and Kerry, and they also owned the present county of Tipperary around Cashel.

In the eleventh and twelfth centuries the MacCarthys had no lands in Cork and Kerry. Their homeland Eoghanacht Cashel was shared with the O'Donoghues and O'Sullivans. Muireadach MacCarthy, son of Carthagh, was King of Eoghanacht Cashel until his death in 1093. Muireadach had two sons, Donough and Cormac, and it was Cormac MacCarthy who succeeded his father as King of Eoghanacht Cashel in 1122 and also became King of Munster. Cormac's reign as King of Munster from 1124 to 1138 was a troubled one because his brother Donough made a claim on the title and he organised revolts among his own people to try and take the crown. Donough was helped in his efforts by Turlogh O'Connor, King of Connaught, and succeeded in dethroning Cormac for a short time. However, Cormac achieved much in his short reign and by building his Church on the Rock of Cashel in 1134 he forged a link between the surname MacCarthy and that historic Seat of the Kings and Bishops of Munster. Cormac MacCarthy's church, still in a perfect state of preservation on the Rock of Cashel, took seven years to build and the Annals record that crowning day of noble achievement — 'A.D. 1134 the Consecration of the Church of Cormac MacCarthy at Cashel by the Archbishop and Bishops of Munster and the Magnates of Ireland, lay and ecclesiastical.' The MacCarthy's power in Desmond was at least due to the desire of the O'Connors of Connaught to set up a conterpoise in Munster to the power of the O'Briens, although Cormac for a greater part of his reign was hostile to the O'Connors and friendly to the O'Briens.

In the year 1138 Cormac MacCarthy was murdered in his own house by treachery' and it is not clear if Donough his brother had any part in this act. However, shortly after his brother's death Donough attempted to become King of Munster, but was captured and handed over to Turlogh O'Brien and died in prison. Cormac's son Dermod soon became King of south Munster aided by the O'Conners of Connaught in defiance of the O'Briens. By 1168 the O'Briens had expelled the MacCarthys from the Eoghanacht of Cashel and had pushed them south into Cork and Kerry.

Dermod MacCarthy was King of Desmond in 1151 and his Kingdom of Cork extended from Lismore, County Waterford, in the east to Brandon Head in Kerry. Dermod MacCarthy had a difficult reign and had varying success against the invaders and was slain in 1185 by Theobald Walter.

Dermod had four sons, Cormac, Donnell Mor, Muircheartach and Tadhg Roe. Cormac rebelled against his father in 1177 and was later slain by the O'Donoghues of Kerry. Muircheartach was killed by the O'Driscolls of Carbery in 1179, and of the two remaining sons, Donnell Mor succeeded Dermod in 1185. It is from this Donnell Mor MacCarthy that most of the many clans of the MacCarthy descend.

Donnell Mor MacCarthy ruled from 1185 to 1206. In 1196 he had a considerable victory over the Anglo-Norman invaders. Donnell Mor was succeeded by his son Dermod Cluasach MacCarthy in 1206 and a period of confusion followed in which various MacCarthys contended for the fast vanishing kingdom. The O'Brien's raids extended to the Lakes of Killarney and far south into County Cork. Dermod Cluasach's reign was significant in making the turning point in the MacCarthy's attitude to the Anglo-Norman invaders. He married a Norman lady, Petronella de Bloot and the Annals tell us that he was on friendly terms with the invaders. Dermod Cluasach MacCarthy died at Dun Droughnan in Muskerry in 1230 and from then on, distinct septs of the MacCarthy clan were formed. Cormac Fionn MacCarthy, second son of Donnell Mor was the first MacCarthy Mor and from him descend all the MacCarthy Mor and the houses of Duhallow and Muskerry, as well as numerous minor clans. From Donnell Gott, third son of Donnell Mor came the great clan of MacCarthy Reigh, Lords of Carbery. In the sixteenth century The MacCarthy Mor ruled over more than 2,000 square miles, and MacCarthy Reigh over more than 600 square miles.

Cormac Fionn died in 1248 and was succeeded by his son Donall Roe MacCarthy (The MacCarthy Mor). In 1251 the Fitzgeralds killed Donall Gott MacCarthy, although

Donall's son Fingin gained a decisive victory over the Geraldines at the Battle of Callan in 1261. Donall Roe established himself as King of Desmond, while the family of Donall Gott directed their energies to the expulsion of the invaders from Carbery. Donall Roe's reign was possibly the most glorious reign of the MacCarthy Clan in Desmond. They captured many castles, such as Dungloe, Macroom, Killorglin, extended their territories up to the borders of west Limerick, recaptured the fertile plains which the invaders occupied, the clans of Duhallow were freed from any dependence on the Geraldines, and the DeCogan and Barretts were driven from the valley of the Lee. Blarney, only seven miles from Cork, became a MacCarthy stronghold.

Donall Oge MacCarthy, son of Donall Roe succeeded his father and the title, The McCarthy Mor, passed on to Donall Oge's son, Cormac Mor. During Cormac's time the power of the MacCarthys in Muskerry increased. They held nearly all of Muskerry north of the Lee, while the O'Learys and O'Mahonys south of the river acknowledged the supremacy of Cormac MacCarthy and his successors. The MacCarthys, under Cormac Mor, as Lords of Muskerry became the wealthiest and most influential of all the descendants of Carthach.

It was Cormac Mor MacCarthy who founded the Friary of Muckross in 1340 and on his death in 1359 he was succeeded by his son Donal Oge II. In 1391 Tadhg Mac-Carthy son of Donal Oge II succeeded his father and completed the Friary at Muckross which was started by his grandfather Cormac.

Tadhg MacCarthy was succeeded by his son Donall Oge III as King of Desmond and was the first Earl of Clancarthy. Tadhg Leith MacCarthy was eventually succeeded by his eldest son Donal in 1489 who reigned 'till 1508 when his brother Cormac Ladhrach MacCarthy claimed the title. In 1517, a year after Cormac's death, The MacCarthy castle on the shores of the Lake of Killarney was taken over by the Geraldines and at this point the power of the Mac-Carthys and Irish was fast declining. Donal MacCarthy, son of Cormac succeeded him and he was succeeded by his son, another Donal. It is during the reign of this Donal from 1565 that the break-up of the old Gaelic order and the establishment of the new Anglo-Irish order began. Donal MacCarthy Mor submitted to Queen Elizabeth, and was made Earl of Clancarthy (or Clancare) and Baron of Valentia. Because Donal had submitted the entire possessions of the MacCarthy Mor had come under English law. Donal MacCarthy had one son Tadhg, Baron of Valentia, and one daughter Ellen by his wife; however, Tadhg predeceased him and thus on Donal's death his illegitimate son Donal assumed the title of MacCarthy Mor, to be succeeded by his son, Donal Oge MacCarthy. However, by English law Ellen was recognised as heiress and Donal Oge was deprived of his properties. At this time Sir Donagh MacCarthy Reagh was Lord of Carbery in Munster and had one son who inherited large tracts of land in Munster and also served for a time in Elizabeth's Army in Munster against the Fitzgeralds, Earls of Desmond. When the power of the Fitzgeralds was finally broken in 1583, Florence went to London to be presented by Queen Elizabeth with an annual stipend for his services. However, his secret marriage to Lady Ellen MacCarthy (daughter of Donal MacCarthy Mor) at Muckross Abbey angered the Queen as it represented a union between the two most formidable branches of the MacCarthy Clan. The English Crown feared the union as a threat to their power in Munster and had Florence arrested and committed to the Tower of London in February 1589. The charge was complicity with Spain against the English Crown. After two years he succeeded in getting released to press counter charges in Ireland against Lord Barry. In 1597 when Donal MacCarthy Mor died and his illegitimate son Donal claimed the title and Florence MacCarthy returned to London to prove his case against that of Donal's for the title of The MacCarthy Mor. The Crown consented to Florence's claim on condition he would be loyal to the Queen's laws in Desmond. Florence arrived back in Ireland in 1599 landing at Cork, and established his camp in Carbery. There he met The O'Neill and asked for his help against Donal. As a result of this

Florence did become the undisputed The MacCarthy Mor and openly defied Carew's officer, Flower, in Carbery. Carew ordered Florence to Cork to explain his actions, promising safe conduct. When Florence arrived in Cork in 1601, however, he was promptly arrested and sent to London. Florence MacCarthy was constantly in and out of prison at the Tower of London between 1601 and 1624. Florence had four sons, Teige who died in his youth; Donal MacCarthy Mor who married Sarah, daughter of the Earl of Antrim; Charles who married Margaret Fitzmaurice daughter of the seventeenth Lord Kerry, and Florence. Having spent most of his life either in prison or in legal battles over his territory in Desmond Florence became embittered in later life, dying in 1640. Lady Ellen, wife of Florence, was recognised as heiress to the greater part of the MacCarthy Mor territory in Kerry. These lands passed to her descendants until in the eighteenth century a Charles MacCarthy Mor left his estates in Killarney to his father-in-law, George Herbert, ancestor of the Herberts of Muckross.

Cormac MacCarthy Oge Lord of Muskerry joined forces with the English in Munster in 1510 against the Fitzgeralds and later led the combined English and Irish forces at Mourne in 1522 when he inflicted a major defeat on the forces of James Fitzgerald, the Earl of Desmond. This defeat reduced the power of the Fitzgeralds in Desmond and yielded the disputed lands to Cormac MacCarthy Oge. He married Catherine Barry, daughter of John Barry, Viscount of Buttervant. He died in 1536 and was buried at Kilcrea. A descendant of Cormac MacCarthy Oge was Sir Cormac MacCarthy who fought on the English side with Lord Carew at the Battle of Kinsale 1602. However, he was secretly corresponding with the Spaniards and the Irish forces under O'Neill and O'Donnell, and was on the point of handing over Blarney Castle to the Irish allied forces when it was discovered and he was arrested. Blarney Castle, together with the Castle at Kilcrea, were taken over by Queen Elizabeth while Sir Charles Wilmot occupied the MacCarthy Castle at Macroom. In the meantime MacCarthy made good his escape from prison and immediately his followers rallied around him, as well as the forces of O'Sullivan Beare from West Carbery. The Crown forces decided that discretion was the better part of valour and a peaceful solution to the conflict was achieved. The MacCarthy Castles and lands at Blarney, Kilcrea and Macroom were returned to Cormac on condition he would keep the peace and support the Queen. He returned to his lands and Castle at Blarney where he died peacefully in February 1616.

Donough MacCarthy, Viscount Muskerry and Earl of Clancarthy devoted most of his life to the defence of his religion and country. If all the MacCarthys were men of war, then Donough was surely the greatest of them. He was appointed General of the Irish forces in Munster in the wars of liberation in 1641 to 1652, and was last to yield to the Cromwelliam forces. In 1652 in a decisive battle with the English Commander Ludlow in Kerry, Donough was defeated surrendering his stronghold Ross Castle and his army of 4,000 men. He was taken to Dublin for trial while his wife and family sought refuge in France. He was acquitted but his large estates were confiscated and he spent many years of exile in France. After the Restoration Donough, now Earl of Clancarthy, was one of the King's followers to benefit from the Act of Settlement. Thanks to James Butler, Duke of Ormond, his brother-in-law, he got back nearly all the Great Muskerry Estates, returning to Ireland to take possession of them in 1659. He died six years later in London.

Because Cormac predeceased his father, his son Cormac Oge became second Earl of Clancarthy at only twleve years old. On his death in 1661 Donough's second son Callaghan became eligible for the title, but was completing his studies for the priesthood in France, Justin, the third son, hoped to become Earl. At this point Callaghan made an unexpected move; attracted by the thought of succeeding, he left the monastery turned Protestant, duly succeeded to the title and property and married Lady Elizabeth Fitzgerald, daughter of the Earl of Kildare.

Realising that the inheritance had slipped away from him

Justin joined the French army. His talents as a soldier were shown to the full when he served under the French General Forenne on the Rhine against the Dutch in 1674. He was appointed by Louvois, Louis XIV's war Minister, to command the foot regiment of the Duke of Monmouth (Charles the Second's illegitimate son) in the Netherlands in 1676. Thanks to the Popish Plot Justin later fell out of favour and it was not until he secretly arranged the wedding of Donough MacCarthy, son of Callaghan MacCarthy, Earl of Clancarthy, to the daughter of Sunderland, the Secretary of State, did his years in the wilderness come to an end. In 1685 he was given a commission to command an Irish regiment of foot, against Protestant criticism. When Charles II died early in 1685 he was succeeded by James II, a Catholic. This change of Kings had a dramatic effect on the army as most of the Protestant Officers were dismissed and replaced by Catholics. However, in 1686 James II promoted Justin Major General and he had secret orders to build a whole new army in Ireland. But at the end of 1688 came the news of William's invasion and James' flight. Justin MacCarthy took effective action against supporters of William in the south of the country, subduing a show of force by Williamite supporters in Bandon. At Castlemartyr he subdued a similar attempt of rebellion.

King James arrived in March 1689 with reinforcements and arms from Louis XIV of France. James was met by Justin MacCarthy and Donough, fourth Earl of Clancarthy at Kinsale. James, after a quick tour of the country, appointed Justin Master General of the Artillery in Ireland and in 1689 he was created Viscount Mountcashel and Baron of Castleinah. Because of the stubborn resistance of the Williamites in Derry and Enniskillen and the failure of De Rosen to breach the defences, James ordered Justin north to finish the sieges. Justin engaged the Enniskilleners under Colonel Wolseley and Colonel Berry at Newtown Butler. Due in part to indiscipline Justin's forces were badly beaten and he was taken prisoner. However, his captivity was short and he escaped to Dublin. He was given a hero's welcome in the capital where James received him.

By now James was seriously considering that a French Brigade in Ireland would be of great help to him, while Louis XIV of France wanted to see the defeat of William at all costs, and was willing to send such a regiment, but he wanted an Irish Brigade to replace it in France. Louis XIV wanted Justin (Lord Mountcashel) to be its commander, however, James was reluctant to lose such a brilliant leader. Mountcashel's personal attributes were quickly noticed by Louis' personal envoy in Ireland, who recognised in Mountcashel qualities of leadership and courage. Mountcashel reformed his own regiment in Cork and organised his brigade. In March 1690 the French Brigade arrived in Cork. It consisted of 6,000 veteran troops, while Mountcashel's Brigade consisted of three regiments, that of Lord Mountcashel, O'Brien and Dillon, with approximately 1,600 men in each regiment, left Ireland. Louis received Mountcashel at Versailles and gave him the rank of Lieutenant-General of France. The Irish Brigade under Mountcashel was immediately committed to General St Ruth in Savoy. The Irish Brigade distinguished themselves in Savoy and captured the enemy of France, the Marquis de Sales. The number of Irish lost in the Savoy campaign was put at 500 fighting men, however, all of Savoy was in their control and Louis XIV was well pleased with Mountcashel.

In 1691 Mountcashel was sent to assist the Duke of Noailles at Catolonia to fight the Spaniards, and in 1693 to the Rhineland front where his regiment was involved in fierce pitched battles, and casualties were high. In 1694, troubled by the wounds that he had received not only on the Continent but in Ireland, he returned to the spa waters of Bareges in the Pyrenees in the hope of curing his wounds, but died there in July 1694 expressing the wish to be buried in Ireland.

Donough MacCarthy, fourth Earl of Clancarthy was born at Blarney Castle in 1668, son of Callaghan MacCarthy, third Earl of Clancarthy, and his wife Elizabeth Fitzgerald, daughter of the Earl of Kildare. During the Jacobite Wars in Ireland he supported James II taking an active part in the events in Munster, alongside his uncle Justin. Taken prisoner at Cork in 1690, he escaped to France having spent four years in the Tower at London. However, having left his wife in England he longed to see her and he secretly crossed the Channel to visit her. He was only in his wife's company for four hours before he was taken and again put in the Tower. He was released on condition he leave the country. He went to Hamburg and bought an island on the Elbe, where he settled with his wife, and, although he was fully pardoned in 1721, he never returned to his home in Ireland.

John George MacCarthy, author and Land Commissioner, was born in Cork in 1829. Educated in Cork, he became a solicitor in 1855. In 1874 he was elected to Parliament in Mallow, as a member of the Irish Parliamentary Party. During his time in Parliament he was deeply involved in the land question. In 1885 he was appointed one of two Commissioners to carry out the Land Purchase Act of that year. Among his many books published were, *The History of Cork 1876, Irish Land Questions, plainly stated and answered, The French Revolution of 1792, its Causes, Events, and Results.* For his work and services to the Catholic Church he was awarded the Order of St Gregory by Pope Leo XIII, and he died in London.

Justin MacCarthy, Irish politician, writer and historian, was born in Cork in 1830. His father was a clerk to the City Magistrates and he wanted Justin to become a lawyer, but he went to work at the local newspaper *The Cork Examiner.*

Justin MacCarthy was an avid member of the Young Ireland Movement, reporting the trials of William Smith O'Brien and

Thomas Francis Megher. He decided that to appeal to the conscience of the English people was the only way to right the wrongs of Ireland to this end he went to England working first with the *Northern Daily Post* at Liverpool. In 1859, having taught himself French, German, Italian, and Spanish, he became foreign editor of the *Morning Star* in London. He started writing novels and eventually resigned from his job and spent a brief time in America. On his return he published a *History of Our Own Times* which was hailed as one of the best literary works of its day. In 1879 he was elected to Parliament for County Longford and was eventually elected Vice-Chairman of the Nationalist Party with Parnell as Chairman. In 1886 he was elected to Parliament as representative for Derry City and in 1892, after the Parnell affair, became Chairman of the Irish Parliamentary Party and continued his policy of advocating Home Rule. He went on writing while leader of the Irish Parliamentary Party, but the constant strain of leadership, coupled with a financial loss he incurred as a member of the Irish Industrial Exhibition in 1894, forced him to give up the Chairmanship to John Dillon. Although he continued in Parliament his health broke down in 1897 and he became almost totally blind. He wrote biographies of Pope Leo XIII and of William Gladstone, and the novels *Lady Judith* published in 1871, and *Dear Lady Disdain* published 1875. Justin MacCarthy could have lived a peaceful life as a successful writer but he preferred to dedicate himself to the service of his country. He died at Folkstone, England in 1912.

Justin MacCarthy's son, Justin Huntly MacCarthy was born in 1861 and followed in his father's footsteps as a writer and a politician. Educated at London Univeristy, his books included an *Outline of Irish History*, 1884; *A History of England under Gladstone;* translations of Omar Khayyan and the Arabian Nights. He also wrote plays; among the better known ones were *The Candidate*, produced in 1882, and *If I Were King* in 1899. He was a Nationalist M.P. from 1884 to 1892 and in 1894 he married the actress Cissie Loftus. He died in 1936 in London.

In more recent years many MacCarthys have excelled in the sporting world. In Gaelic Games two MacCarthys have distinguished themselves in their native Cork colours. Gerald MacCarthy of St Finbarrs Hurling Club is probably one of the greatest exponents of hurling. He had the unique distinction of being the only player ever to captain his county to senior and under twenty-one All Ireland Hurling Championships in one year — 1966.

Charlie MacCarthy of Cork (who won three All-Ireland medals with his county team in 1966, 1970, and 1976) is noted for his spectacular skill and speed with the hurley.

Jim MacCarthy, now a successful businessman, has brought honour to his native Cork and to the Province of Munster in Rugby. Capped twenty-six times for the National Team he was considered one of the greatest wing-forwards Ireland ever produced. He played on the team that won the Triple Crown in 1948 and took a significant part in helping Ireland to their victory.

THE MacCARTHYS OF LEINSTER AND ULSTER

MacCarthy is primarily a Munster surname, although it is now found in all four provinces.

Denis Florence MacCarthy, National scholar and poet, was born in Dublin in 1817 and was educated at Trinity College. His parents wanted him to study for the priesthood but Florence interested himself in law and he was called to the Bar in 1846. He never practised but devoted himself to poetry and literature. His first verses were published in the *Dublin Satirist* when

he was seventeen years of age. Later he contributed to
the *Dublin University Magazine* and to *The Nation* under
the pseudonym of 'Desmond'. He wrote mostly on Irish
patriotic themes, and his songs were of high standard; his
poems unmistakably Irish in style and conception. He felt
his mission as a poet with a fervour equal to that of any
contributor to 'The Spirit of the Nation'

> There's not a man of all our land
> Our country now can spare
> The strong man with his sinewy hand
> The weak man with his prayer.
> No whining tone of mere regret
> Young Irish Bards for you
> But let your songs teach Ireland yet
> What Irishmen should do.

In 1854 he was appointed Professor of Literature in
the Catholic University of Dublin. In the next few years
he directed his attention to Spanish literature and in 1881
the Royal Academy of Spain presented MacCarthy with a
medal in recognition of the service he had rendered to
Spanish Literature. When he died in 1882 he was considered one of the greatest poets of the Young Ireland
Movement.

The Rt. Rev Wilbor MacCarthy was born in Dublin in
1841 and educated at Trinity College where he received
his Doctorate in Divinity. He was twenty-six when he
took holy orders, and shortly after left for India as a
missionary. In 1892 he was created Archdeacon of Cal-
cutta, and in 1905 consecrated Bishop of Grantham. He
died in London in 1925.

In Ulster the surname MacCarthy is more widely found
in its variant form of MacCartney. General George Mac-
Cartney, born in Belfast in 1660, was a flamboyant
character, entering the army and was rapdily promoted. He
was appointed a Colonel in 1703 and in 1706 saw action
in Flanders at Ostend. In 1707 while fighting in Spain as
Brigadier he was captured, but later released in an exchange

of prisoners. In 1709 Queen Ann dismissed him from the army for his insulting behaviour towards an old woman in London under the influence of drink. In the famous duel fought in Hyde Park in 1712 between Lord Mohan and the Duke of Hamilton he acted as second to Lord Mohan, and Colonel John Hamilton acted as second to the Duke. The final result of the duel was that both contestants were mortally wounded; however, it was alleged that Mac-Cartney slew the wounded Duke after the duel and Colonel Hamilton swore to this. MacCartney fled to Holland after the Duchess of Hamilton had issued a notice of reward leading to his capture. In 1714 after the death of Queen Ann, MacCartney returned and gave himself up; whereupon he was tried for murder. However, Colonel Hamilton now wavered in his previous evidence and MacCartney was acquitted. He was restored to his army rank of Colonel. In 1717 he was promoted to Lieutenant General, and in 1722 was promoted to General commanding the army in Ireland. He died in 1730 aged seventy.

THE MacCARTHYS IN ENGLAND

Many MacCarthys of Irish emigrant families have distinguished themselves in different aspects of life in England.

In the British Navy in the eighteenth century a sailor on *H.M.S. Inflexible* called John MacCarthy led a mutiny against the appalling conditions in the navy at the time. King George III was on the throne of England and was much embarrassed by the action, which forced the fleet to sail into French and Spanish ports. The welfare of the sailors was immediately improved as a result.

The renowned actress Lillah MacCarthy was born in Cheltenham in September 1875 of an Irish father and English mother. She made her stage debut as Lady Macbeth at St Georges Hall in 1895 and in 1896 she played Mercia in *The Sign of the Cross* at the Lyric Theatre. This established her as a dramatic actress. Her velvet voice and tall statuesque appearance created a great impression on the stage. In 1906 she married the producer Granville-Barker with whom she had worked for the previous three years. The marriage did not last long and but, for the support of Shaw who encouraged her to continue acting, she would have left the stage. In 1920 she married Sir Frederick Keeble and in April 1932 had the honour of being the first actress to speak on the opening of the Shakespeare Memorial Theatre, at Stratford-on-Avon. Her Autobiography *Myself and My Friends* was published in 1933. She was eighty-five years of age when she died in 1960 in London.

Sir Desmond MacCarthy was a noted writer and literary critic. Born in Plymouth in 1877, educated at Eton and Cambridge. His first job was writing reviews for *The Speaker* and in 1904 he became dramatic critic for the paper. From 1907 to 1910 he edited the *New Quarterly* and in 1913 became the dramatic critic of the *New Statesmen and Nation.* While there he wrote under the pen name Affable Hawk, which aptly described his sharp criticisms and his warm character. His career with the *New Statesman* was temporarily interrupted to serve in the Red Cross during his first World War. He left the *New Statesman* in 1928 to become senior literary critic with the *Sunday Times* which position he held until he died. He wrote about literary figures he had known like Shaw, Ruskin, Asquith, and Conrad. Thanks to these writings he established a reputation in America. He was knighted in 1951 and the following year received a honorary doctorate from Cambridge. He died shortly after.

In 1916, when Shackleton attempted to cross the Antartic Sea from shore to shore he had with him one Timothy MacCarthy. During that great Antartic expedition their ship *Endurance* sank and Shackleton, together with Tim MacCarthy and four others sailed to safety more than 800 miles in an open boat.

In more recent times Paul McCartney, M.B.E., song-writer and member of The Beatles bears a variant of the name with distinction. Born in Liverpool in 1942, he showed his interest in music at an early age and taught himself to play the guitar, piano, organ and trumpet. The Beatles were formed in 1960, and they captured the imagination of teenagers all over the world. The four Beatles — who included McCartney — sold a staggering 545 million copies of their records in twelve years up to 1972. Some of their music was composed by McCartney and after the group disbanded in 1972 he continued to compose and perform on his own. He was given an M.B.E. in the British Honours list of 1968.

THE MacCARTHYS IN EUROPE

In 1690 Justin MacCarthy, Lord Mountcashel, sailed from Cork Harbour with the first Irish Brigade to serve in the armies of Louis XIV, King of France. This Brigade was the first of many which saw Irish soldiers going into exile to fight for the armies of Europe. These fighting men became known as the Wild Geese. Although Justin Mac-Carthy distinguished himself and Louis XIV made him Lieutenant-General of France, many more MacCarthys were among the rank and file of the Irish Brigades, and fought in major battles in Holland, Belgium, Germany, and Spain. There are descendants of the MacCarthys still living in these countries today. There are some interesting derivations of the MacCarthy surname in evidence in Europe. Among the most numerous are: Macarni, Macarti, Macarru, Cari, Corri, and Corru.

Justin, Count MacCarthy, who was born at Spring House in County Tipperary went to France in 1774 and settled in Toulouse. He had a collection of books and he assembled at his home in Toulouse, now a hotel, the largest library in all France. He is said to have paid the highest price ever given for a printed book up to the eighteenth century.

In the church affairs of France the MacCarthys also left their mark, Nicholas MacCarthy, born in Dublin in 1769, was educated in France and showed remarkable ability in philosophy and Hebrew. During the Revolution he retired to Toulouse and was a late vocation for the priesthood, being ordained in 1814. His powers of oratory were superb, and he could speak with authority on many varied subjects due to knowledge acquired from abnormal periods of study. The Revolution of 1830 forced him to leave France and go to Italy. In 1833 he died at the bishop's residence in Annecy and was buried in the Cathedral.

Another churchman whose remains lie in a Cathedral in Europe was Bishop Thaddeus MacCarthy, Bishop of Cork and Cloyne. His remains lie at Ivrea in France. Thaddeus, who studied at Kilcrea in west Cork, was appointed Bishop of Ross by Pope Sixtus IV but a Hugh O'Driscoll who had been auxiliary to the previous Bishop disputed the decision and sought to have him removed. Pope Innocent VII settled the dispute by declaring Hugh O'Driscoll Bishop of Ross and Thaddeus MacCarthy Bishop of Cork and Cloyne, but his enemies continued to intrigue against Bishop Mac-Carthy and would not allow him to take up his duties. Thaddeus went to Rome to seek support from the Pope, and Alexander VI confirmed his appointment. On his way back, worn out after many years of defending his rights he stopped at Ivrea at the foot of the Alps. There at the hospice called the Twenty-One Thaddeus MacCarthy, Bishop of Cork and Cloyne, died. A bright light was seen by many over his bed on his death. He was beatified in 1896.

The MacCarthy women were also prominent on the Continent of Europe. Marianne MacCarthy and her husband Dominingo O Mourogho (Murphy) were compelled to leave Ireland and find a new home in Spain. It must be said that the Spanish Monarchy were very loyal and friendly to the Irish down through our sad history; far more hospitable than any other nations we served. During the journey to Spain a child was born to Marianne, and on her arrival in Spain she was immediately welcomed into the Spanish Court. Taken by the beauty of the boy, the Queen appointed the Court as guardian of the child and provided him with a special tutor and awarded his parents a pension for life.

Sir Charles MacCarthy was born in France in 1770 and was an officer in the Irish Brigade up to the time of the Revolution. In 1794 he entered the British Army and, after service in the West Indies, was promoted to Captain in 1796. Later he was promoted to command of the Royal African Corps in 1811. In 1812 he was made Governor of Sierra Leone and was responsible for administering the territories of Ghana (then the Gold Coast) and Nigeria. He was knighted in 1820 and was promoted to Colonel in 1821. He fought many small battles with the war like Ashantees, but during a major campaign against them in 1824 he was mortally wounded. So great was his enemies respect for his courage that they removed his head and preserved it as a relic of military prowess. It is held in the Sacred Groves of Ashanti to this day.

THE MacCARTHYS IN AMERICA

Many MacCarthys have contributed to the formation and growth of the new world. In the early years before America achieved its independance the surname MacCarthy was familiar to the citizens of Boston, for in 1684 Thade MacCarthy was Town Constable of that city.

In 1873 Charles MacCarthy, the political scientist, was born in Brockton, Massachusetts. His father, John MacCarthy, and his mother, Katherine O'Shea, were both emigrant Irish who had settled in Brockton and worked in a shoe factory there. Charles had a tough upbringing. He sold newspapers, worked in the docks, and did similar jobs. He supported himself through College working on odd jobs at night and having received a primary degree at the Univeristy of Georgia he received his Ph.D. in Political Science from the University of Wisconsin in 1899, and his thesis won the highest award of the American Historical Association. His eloquence, his agile brain and decisive writing made him a great influence during his lifetime, and he had great influence on successive American Presidents and, indeed, on political life generally. Charles MacCarthy founded the first official reference library and Bill-drafting office in America for legislators, at Madison, Wisconsin. In 1914 he was appointed the first Director of the United States Commission on Industrial Relations. He died in Prescott Arizona in 1921.

In 1917, the year America entered the First World War, Colonel Daniel E. MacCarthy was the first American soldier of the Expeditionary Force to set foot in France.

MacCarthyism was a word coined by the American Press when reporting the activities of one Senator, Joseph MacCarthy. He was born in 1909 on a farm at Appleton, Wisconsin. After a chequered school career he graduated in Law from Marquette University. He became a Circuit Judge, but when World War II broke out he enlisted in the Marines and spent most of his military career in the South Pacific as an intelligence officer. After the War he contested the Senate Seat in Wisconsin against the sitting Senator, Bob Lafellette. MacCarthy beat Lafellette by a substantial margin in one of the major political upsets of 1946. For several years the United States Congress had been trying to use its powers under the Constitution to force the Executive Branch of the Government to clean out the communist influences. On 9 February, 1950 Senator Joseph MacCarthy demanded direct interrogation of alleged suspects. That which Senator Joseph MacCarthy started in 1950 and finished in 1954 was to become known as MacCarthyism throughout the United States. Because of the fervour with which he pursued alleged communists he was himself attacked and his political career was permanently destroyed.

Mary MacCarthy, the American novelist and short story writer was born in 1912 in Seattle of Irish-Jewish parents. Both died when she was only six and together with her three younger brothers Mary MacCarthy was brought up by her uncle. When she completed her studies at Vasser University, she began to write book reviews for *The Nation* and the *New Republic*. She has written many novels and short stories, and won

many literary awards for her works, which include *The Oasis* (a novel), *The Writing on The Wall* (essays), *Cast a Cold Eye* (short stories), *The Group* (novel) — later filmed.

Kevin MacCarthy, her brother, is a film actor of note and distinguished himself in such films as *The Prize, Operation Heartbeat* and *Kansas City Bomber.*

Politician Eugene MacCarthy, the well-known Democrat, was born in 1916 in Watkins, Minnesota, and after his initial education in his local town, he graduated from Minnesota University, majoring in Economics. During the war he was an assistant to the Army's War Department, and after the war pursued an academic career, becoming Professor of Economics at St John's University, Minnesota. In 1948 he entered politics and was elected to the House of Representatives, where he remained until 1958 when he was elected to Congress as Senator for Minnesota, which position he held until 1971. In 1955 he was given an honorary degree for Literature at St Louis University. Amongst his published works are *Frontiers in American Democracy,* 1960, *Dictionary of American Politics,* 1962, *The Limits of Power,* and *America's Role in the World,* 1967. Eugene MacCarthy unsuccessfully sought the Democratic Presidential nomination in 1968 against Hubert Humphreys.

SUGGESTED READING

A History of Surnames of the British Isles, C. Lestrange Ewen. London 1931.

A Guide to Irish Surnames, Edward MacLysaght. Dublin 1964.

American Origins, L. G. Pine. New York 1960.

Burkes Landed Gentry of Ireland, Burkes Peerage Ltd. London 1912.

Facts about Ireland, Dept of External Affairs. Dublin 1963.

Guide to Irish Genealogy, Irish Genealogical Research Society. London 1966.

Handbook on Irish Genealogy, Heraldic Artists Ltd. Dublin 1976.

In Search of Ancestry, Gerald Hamilton-Edwards. London 1974.

Illustrated Ireland Guide, Bord Failte Eireann. Dublin 1967.

Irish Families, Edward MacLysaght. Dublin 1957.

Paper Extracts, Guildhall Library London.

Surnames and Christian Names in Ireland, R. E. Matheson. London 1901.

Spanish Knights of Irish Origin, Micheline Walsh. Dublin 1960.

Surnames, Ernest Weekley, M.A. London 1916.

The Irish in America, W. D. Griffin. New York 1973.

Thomas Davis and Young Ireland, M. J. MacManus. Dublin 1945.

Wild Geese in Spanish Flanders, B. Jennings. Dublin 1964.

Blarney Castle: seat of the MacCarthy's of Muskerry.